A Handbook of Spiritual Ecumenism

A Handbook of Spiritual Ecumenism

Cardinal Walter Kasper

New City Press
Hyde Park, New York

Published in the United States by New City Press
202 Cardinal Rd., Hyde Park, NY 12538
www.newcitypress.com
©2007 Cardinal Walter Kasper

Cover design by Durva Correia

Library of Congress Cataloging-in-Publication Data:
A catalog record is available from the Library of Congress

ISBN-13: 978-1-56548-263-0

1st printing: November 2006
3rd printing: November 2008

Printed in the United States of America

A special acknowledgement to
Monsignor Johan Bonny and Fr Donald Bolen
for their extensive contributions
to the preparation of this handbook.

Contents

To the Reader

The search for unity among Christians is, before all else, a desire to be kept alive and a prayer to be nourished. This search has its eyes fixed on Jesus, who gave his life so that there would be "one flock, one shepherd" (Jn 10:16) and who prayed "that they may all be one" (Jn 17:21). Many have come to understand that if it doesn't go back to its moorings, ecumenical engagement risks losing its *elan,* its hope; it risks coming to a standstill in the face of human limitations.

I am happy to be able to present this handbook on spiritual ecumenism, the soul of the ecumenical movement. This text is the fruit of stimulating experiences in which I have been able to take part over the past years. It also has taken shape thanks to the contribution of numerous people and groups who have wished to share their lived experience and their intuitions in the domain of spiritual ecumenism. I offer it as a practical aid — and as a heartfelt invitation — addressed to all who have taken to heart the cause of unity among Christians. My hope is that it may help us to be ever more closely united with our brothers and sisters in a common prayer around Christ, our one Lord.

Preface

A Handbook

1. This booklet offers practical suggestions aimed at implementing and strengthening that spiritual ecumenism which is the heart of all efforts to bring divided Christians together again in unity. It finds its origin in the 2003 Plenary Meeting of the Pontifical Council for Promoting Christian Unity, which focused on the theme of "spiritual ecumenism."[1] During this session the bishops recommended that a brief handbook or *Vademecum* be produced, inviting those having special responsibility in promoting Christian unity to deepen the spiritual roots of ecumenism and offering suggestions to this end. In November 2004, a draft version was set forward for discussion at an international conference in Rocca di Papa, organized by the Pontifical Council for Promoting Christian Unity on the occasion of the fortieth anniversary celebration of the Second Vatican Council's Decree *Unitatis Redintegratio*.

---

1. Cf. Pontifical Council for Promoting Christian Unity, Information Service (IS), n. 115 (2004/I-II), pp. 23-39.

Based on suggestions from participants and subsequent proposals made available by local ecumenical bodies, the present text was prepared for publication.

2. This handbook is grounded in the documents of the Second Vatican Council, especially in *Dei Verbum*,[2] *Lumen Gentium*,[3] *Unitatis Redintegratio*[4] and *Orientalium Ecclesiarum*,[5] and in later documents that have further shaped the Catholic Church's engagement in seeking Christian unity, including the Codes of Canon Law,[6] the Encyclical Letter *Ut Unum Sint*,[7] the *Catechism of the Catholic Church*,[8] and particularly the *Directory for the Application of Principles and Norms on Ecumenism*.[9]

Applying the teaching, guidelines and norms of these documents to the domain of spiritual ecumenism is the central purpose of this text. The pastoral suggestions that it offers flow from this extensive corpus of Church teaching on the promotion of Christian unity.

---

2. Second Vatican Council, Dogmatic Constitution on Divine Revelation *Dei Verbum* (DV), 1965.
3. Second Vatican Council, Dogmatic Constitution on the Church *Lumen Gentium* (LG), 1964.
4. Second Vatican Council, Decree on Ecumenism *Unitatis Redintegratio* (UR), 1964.
5. Second Vatican Council, Decree on Eastern Catholic Churches *Orientalium Ecclesiarum* (OE), 1964.
6. Both the *Code of Canon Law* (CIC), 1983, and the *Code of Canon Law of the Eastern Churches* (CCEO), 1990.
7. Pope John Paul II, Encyclical Letter *Ut Unum Sint* (UUS), 1995.
8. *Catechism of the Catholic Church* (CCC), 1994.
9. Pontifical Council for Promoting Christian Unity, *Directory for the Application of Principles and Norms on Ecumenism* (Directory), 1993.

3. This handbook is addressed to everyone who has at heart the restoration of unity among Christians. It can be helpful in particular to those in charge of promoting Christian unity at various levels of Church life. In drawing on the resources in this handbook, they will need to be mindful that what is suitable in some contexts may be inappropriate in others; what is helpful in one place may be counterproductive elsewhere. In light of local circumstances and of decisions taken at regional or national levels, this discernment is to be carried out under the guidance of the local bishop, who is to shepherd the people of God in finding and fostering the means by which Christian unity can be constructively promoted in his diocese.[10]

In issuing this text, we extend a loving invitation to Christians of other traditions, encouraging them to join with their Catholic brothers and sisters in the prayer and spiritual activities recommended in this document, insofar as these are in keeping with their own practice. Each time we engage in common prayer, each act of common witness, indeed every act of spiritual communion is a gift of the Holy Spirit, who binds us together and enables us to give visible expression to our Lord's desire for unity.

---

10. Cf. UR, n. 8; Directory, n. 164.

Spiritual Ecumenism

> *"This change of heart and holiness of life, along with public and private prayer for the unity of Christians, should be regarded as the soul of the whole ecumenical movement, and merits the name 'spiritual ecumenism.' "*[11]

4. On the eve of his suffering and death, Jesus prayed *"that they may all be one. As you, Father, are in me and I in you, may they also be one in us, so that the world may believe that you have sent me"* (Jn 17:21). It is significant that Jesus did not primarily express his desire for unity in a teaching or in a commandment to his disciples, but in a prayer to his Father. Unity is a gift from above, stemming from and growing toward loving communion with the Father, Son and Holy Spirit. Christian prayer for unity is a humble but faithful sharing in the prayer of Jesus, who promised that any prayer in His name would be heard by the Father.[12]

5. Spiritual ecumenism finds its expression in *"public and private prayer for the unity of Christians."* Since unity is a gift, it is fitting that Christians pray for it together: *"Such prayers in common are certainly a very effective means of petitioning for the*

---

11. UR, n. 8; cf. Directory, n. 63.
12. Cf. Jn 15:7.

grace of unity, and they are a genuine expression of the ties which even now bind Catholics to their separated brethren. 'For where two or three are gathered together for my sake, there am I in the midst of them' (Mt 18:20)."[13] Prayer for unity is the royal door of ecumenism: it leads Christians to look at the Kingdom of God and the unity of the Church in a fresh way; it deepens their bonds of communion; and it enables them to courageously face painful memories, social burdens and human weakness. In every age of history, the principal artisans of reconciliation and unity were persons of prayer and contemplation, inspiring divided Christians to recommit themselves to walk the path of unity.

6. Spiritual ecumenism also requires a *"change of heart and holiness of life,"* arising from Jesus' call to conversion.[14] The way toward reconciliation and communion unfolds when Christians feel the painful wound of division in their hearts, in their minds and in their prayers. This experience makes them aware of how much harm has been caused by pride and selfishness, by polemics and condemnations, by disdain and presumption. It also awakens in them a readiness to engage in a serious examination of conscience, recognizing their faults and trusting in the reconciling power of the Gospel. Only in the context of conversion

---

13. UR, n. 8; cf. UUS, n. 21 f.
14. Cf. Mk 1:14-15; UR, n. 7; UUS, n. 15 f., 33 f., 84 f.

and renewal of mind can the wounded bonds of communion be healed.[15]

7. Spiritual ecumenism, finally, is called *"the soul of the whole ecumenical movement."* According to the Second Vatican Council, the ecumenical movement has been brought about *"under the inspiring grace of the Holy Spirit."*[16] It is a spiritual process, carried out in faithful obedience to the Father, following the will of Christ, under the guidance of the Holy Spirit. The work of ecumenism, therefore, is rooted in the foundations of Christian spirituality, requiring more than ecclesial diplomacy, academic dialogue, social involvement and pastoral cooperation. It presupposes a real appreciation of the many elements of sanctification and truth wrought by the Holy Spirit both within and beyond the visible boundaries of the Catholic Church. The words of the psalm apply to the endeavor to foster Christian unity: *"Unless the Lord builds the house, those who build it labor in vain. Unless the Lord watches over the city, the watchman stays awake in vain"* (Ps 127:1).

---

15. Cf. UUS, n. 82.
16. UR, n. 4; cf. UR, n. 1.

Growing in Communion

"For those who believe in Christ and have been properly baptized are put in a certain though imperfect communion with the Catholic Church. The differences that exist in varying degrees between them and the Catholic Church — whether in doctrine and sometimes in discipline, or concerning the structure of the Church — do indeed create many obstacles, sometimes serious ones, to full ecclesiastical communion. The ecumenical movement is striving to overcome these obstacles."[17]

8. Christians can say with joy and gratitude that *"what unites us is much greater than what divides us."*[18] All Christians profess faith in God the Father Almighty, in Jesus Christ, Son of God and Savior, and in the Holy Spirit, the Advocate, the Giver of life and holiness. Through the sacrament of Baptism they are reborn and united with Christ. They honor sacred Scripture as the Word of God and as an abiding norm of belief and action. They share in prayer and draw upon many other common sources of the spiritual life. Many Christians rejoice in the episcopate, celebrate the Eucharist and cultivate devotion to

---

17. UR, n. 3; cf. CCC, n. 820-822; 836-838; Directory, n. 9-21.
18. UUS, n. 20, quoting Pope John XXIII.

Mary, the Virgin Mother of God.[19] The sancti-
fying power of the Holy Spirit is operative among
all of them, strengthening them in holiness. It is
the Holy Spirit who has given courage to Christians of many traditions as they have faced persecution, even to the point of martyrdom. These
elements of communion *"which come from Christ
and lead back to Him, belong by right to the one Church
of Christ."*[20]

9. The Second Vatican Council primarily un-
derstands the Church as communion. It teaches
that the Church of Christ *"subsists in the Catholic
Church"* — while recognizing that outside of the
visible boundaries of the Catholic Church *"many
elements of sanctification and of truth can be found,"*
which *"as gifts properly belonging to the Church of
Christ, possess an inner dynamism toward Catholic
unity."*[21] The Church of Christ is not a prospec-
tive future reality, still to be realized; it already
exists in a concrete historical form. This is also
true for the unity of the Church, which the Catholic Church believes to subsist in it *"as something
she can never lose and that we hope will continue to
increase, until the end of time."*[22] Though not in full
communion with the Catholic Church, other
Churches and Ecclesial Communities retain in

19. Cf. UUS, n. 12.
20. UR, n. 3; cf. UUS, n. 13; CCC, n. 817-819.
21. LG, n. 8; cf. UUS, n. 10.
22. UR, n. 4; cf. UUS, n. 14.

reality a certain communion with it, in varying degrees. This ecclesiology of communion is the context for understanding and nurturing ecumenism, directed to *"making the partial communion existing between Christians grow toward full communion in truth and charity."*[23]

10. Certain features of the Christian mystery have at times been more effectively emphasized by other Churches or Ecclesial Communities.[24] The Holy Spirit has enriched them with particular ways of reading and meditating upon the sacred Scripture, diverse forms of public worship and private devotion, differing expressions of Christian witness and holiness of life. All these treasures in East and West, in North and South, can rightly be valued as gifts of the Holy Spirit to the one Church of Christ: *"Whatever is wrought by the grace of the Holy Spirit in the hearts of our separated brethren can contribute to our own edification."*[25]

11. By sharing in these spiritual treasures, the Catholic Church can better express in actual life its full catholicity and further deepen its understanding of the means of sanctification entrusted to it by the Lord. This "exchange of gifts" is one of the ways for the Holy Spirit to guide the Church *"into all the truth"* (Jn 16:13). Christians need

---

23. UUS, n. 14; cf. Bibliography: Ecumenical documents on the Church.
24. Cf. UUS, n. 14.
25. UR, n. 4.

therefore to be invited and encouraged to jointly participate in spiritual activities, to make use of common resources, to do together all that is possible in a manner and to a degree appropriate to the present level of agreement.[26]

---

26. Cf. UR, n. 8.

1
Deepening
Christian Faith

The Word of God in Sacred Scripture

"Veneration of the Scriptures is a fundamental bond of unity between Christians, one that holds firm even when the Churches and Communities to which they belong are not in full communion with each other. Everything that can be done to make members of the Churches and Ecclesial Communities read the Word of God, and to do that together when possible (e.g., Bible Weeks), reinforces this bond of unity that already unites them, helps them to be open to the unifying action of God and strengthens the common witness to the saving Word of God which they give to the world."[1]

12. Out of the abundance of His love, God, who is invisible, *"speaks to humankind as friends and enters into their life, so as to invite and receive them into relationship with himself."*[2] The Church receives the one deposit of the Word of God through sacred Tradition and sacred Scripture together. It also has been entrusted with the task of authentically interpreting the Word of God and with a teaching function that *"is not above the Word of God but stands at its service, teaching nothing but what is*

---

1. Directory, n. 183; cf. UR, n. 21.
2. DV, n. 2.

handed down, according as it devotedly listens, reverently preserves and faithfully transmits the Word of God, by divine command and with the help of the Holy Spirit."[3]

13. The Word of God in sacred Scripture has a central place in the life and mission of the Church. It is first of all in the liturgy of the Church that sacred Scripture is venerated, read and explained. All preaching must be nourished and ruled by it. Sacred Scripture also strengthens the life of the faithful, as *"food for the soul"* and source of spiritual life.[4] The Catholic Church, therefore, seeks to promote easy access to sacred Scripture for all and sees to it that suitable and correct translations are made available in different languages.[5] It encourages biblical scholars to explore and to explain the sacred writings, following the mind of the Church,[6] for *"the study of the sacred page is, as it were, the soul of sacred theology."*[7] Finally, the faithful are urged to deepen their knowledge of Jesus Christ by frequent reading of the Scriptures, for *"ignorance of the Scriptures is ignorance of Christ."*[8] Though many fruitful efforts have already been made, Catholics are further encouraged to receive

---

3. DV, n. 10.
4. Cf. DV, n. 21.
5. Cf. DV, n. 22.
6. Cf. DV, n. 23.
7. DV, n. 24.
8. DV, n. 25, quoting St. Jerome, *Commentary on Isaiah*, PL 24,17.

"the bread of life from the one table of God's Word and Christ's Body."[9]

14. The Word of God in sacred Scripture enlightens and nourishes Christians of all traditions. The Second Vatican Council affirms that the authentic theological traditions of the Eastern Churches *"are admirably rooted in Holy Scripture."*[10] As to the Churches and Ecclesial Communities in the West, the Council states that they have *"a love and reverence"* of sacred Scriptures and that *"calling upon the Holy Spirit, they seek in these sacred Scriptures God as He speaks to them in Christ, the One whom the prophets foretold, God's Word made flesh for us."*[11] The Catholic Church considers sacred Scripture therefore as *"an instrument of the highest value in the mighty hand of God for the attainment of that unity which the Savior holds out to all."*[12] How can sacred Scripture increasingly be used as *"an instrument of the highest value"* along the path of Christian unity?

"Lectio Divina"

Christians can come to a deeper familiarity with the sacred text through a prayerful reading of sacred Scripture or *"lectio divina."* The first purpose of this reading is spiritual: welcoming the loving presence and voice of God, finding food for

---

9. Cf. DV, n. 21.
10. UR, n. 17.
11. UR, n. 21.
12. Ibid.

the soul, discerning the will of God and growing in obedience to it.[13] This reading of sacred Scripture becomes an intimate dialogue with God, for *"when we pray, we talk to Him; when we read the Divine Word, we listen to Him."*[14]

15. Together, Christians can

- read and meditate upon particular books of sacred Scripture in small groups, as part of a shared spiritual journey;
- make available reading lists of passages from sacred Scripture for reflection by Christians of different traditions, individually or in groups;[15]
- publish together commentaries on sacred Scripture, drawing from the writings or teachings of spiritual leaders and scholars of various traditions;
- conduct Bible courses, organized by and conducted together with neighboring parish communities.

---

13. Cf. CCC, n. 1177; 2705-2708.
14. DV, n. 25, quoting St. Ambrose, *On the duties of Ministers*, I,20,88: PL 16,50.
15. E.g., the monthly *"Word of Life"* issued for all members and friends of the Focolare Movement; the monthly *"Meditating on the Word"* forwarded with the *"Letter of Taizé"* to all friends of the Community of Taizé; the *"Daily Watchwords"* of the Moravian Church; calendars with scriptural quotations for each day of the year.

Common Bible Work

16. In many regions, there is a well-established practice of working together on Bible-related projects, which has been much appreciated as an accessible and fruitful means of promoting Christian unity. Meritorious efforts have been made, thanks to the ecumenical cooperation of scholars belonging to various traditions, in the preparation and publication of commonly agreed Bible translations and editions.[16] These efforts are a valuable form of common service and common witness which could be expanded.[17]

Together, Christians can

- organize specific days, weeks or years dedicated to the Bible or to biblical themes, e.g. a "Bible Sunday" for parishes, a "Bible Day" for families, a "Bible Week" for children or youth, a "Year of the Bible" on the level of dioceses;
- publish Bible study resources for use in local congregations, adapted to various groups in the community (e.g., children, youth, elderly, women, families, social commitment groups);

---

16. Cf. *"Guidelines for Interconfessional Cooperation in Translating the Bible"* (new revised edition 1987 of the first 1968 version), in: IS, n. 65 (1987/III-IV), pp. 140-145.
17. On the role of the *Catholic Biblical Federation* and the *United Bible Societies*, cf. Directory, n. 184-185.

- explore the possibility of using common scriptural readings for liturgical purposes;[18]
- face together the growing biblical illiteracy among many Christians and the spiritual thirst of many for the "Word of Life," by offering appropriate resources;
- work together in the preparation of biblical programs or resources for audiovisual and electronic media, using easily accessible formats (TV, CD-Rom, DVD).

Common Understanding of Sacred Scripture

17. According to their doctrinal traditions, Churches and Ecclesial Communities developed different ways of understanding and using the sacred Scripture. When reading together the Bible, Christians begin to come to terms with their distinct confessional approaches to it. Common Bible work can allow them to better understand *"the relationship between sacred Scripture, as the highest authority in matters of faith, and sacred Tradition, as indispensable to the interpretation of the Word of God."*[19]

---

18. Cf. Directory, n. 187.
19. UUS, n. 79.

Together, Christians can

- face directly those scriptural texts that have given rise to disagreements, especially those passages that have special significance for a particular tradition; while remaining loyal to the teaching of their own faith communities, they can grow in mutual understanding and gain appreciation for the ways others have approached the Word of God;[20]

- gain new insights into different ways of reading Scripture. Diverse ecclesial traditions in East and West have given a privileged place at times to more literal, symbolic, theological or mystagogical understandings of sacred Scripture; working together, Christians can come to value the respective merits of these approaches and their possible complementarity;

- engage in joint witness as they respond to questions and issues raised by modern society, especially moral matters (human rights, the beginning and the end of human life, human sexuality, marriage and family life, war and peace, terrorism and security, poverty and justice) in light of the Word of God, as it comes to us through sacred Scripture and the Church's tradition.[21]

20. Cf. Directory, n. 186.
21. Ibid.

Sacred Scripture and Church Unity

18. Coming together to read and to study
sacred Scripture, attention can be paid to the
mystery of unity and division as it unfolds in the
history of salvation. Many passages of different
literary genres (historic texts, psalms and prayers,
prophetic sayings, teachings, parables) in both
Old and New Testaments are particularly relevant
from that point of view.

Common reading of sacred Scripture can usefully
focus on:
- the loving unity of the Father, the Son and
  the Holy Spirit and their divine reconciling
  activity in the origins and the life of the
  Church;[22]
- the painful reality of division: its origin
  in human fragility and sinfulness, its profound
  and lasting effects, its crying out to God and
  searching for words in prayer, its longing for
  forgiveness and reconciliation;[23]
- the teaching of Jesus on the Kingdom of
  God, which He revealed and inaugurated in
  his words and deeds, and which, after his
  death and resurrection, the Church has

---

22. Cf. LG, n. 2-4; cf. Jn 16:4-15; Eph 4:1-16.
23. E.g. Gen 4:1-16 (Cain and Abel); Gen 37-50 (the history of
    Joseph); Is 42-53 (songs of the suffering servant); Ps 44 (lament
    and prayer for help); Mk 9:33-40 (Who is the greatest?); Lk
    12:51-53 (Jesus the cause of division); Lk 15 (the parables of the
    lost sheep, the lost coin and the prodigal son).

been commissioned to proclaim among all peoples;[24]

- Jesus' expressed desire for the unity of his disciples, and the subsequent teaching of the apostles and their constant endeavour to safeguard the unity of the Church when threatened by internal or external powers of discord and division;[25]

- the images or symbols used in the Bible for describing the nature or mystery of the Church:[26] Old Testament images relating to *"the people of God"*;[27] New Testament images centered on Christ as head of the Church, which is his Body;[28] images taken from daily life, such as the shepherd and his flock,[29] the cultivation of land (like the vineyard and the vinedresser)[30], the art of building (like the edifice or temple and the living stones,[31] the Jerusalem which comes from above),[32] and marriage or family life (like the bride of Christ[33] and the family of God).[34]

---

24. Cf. LG, n. 5; cf. Mk 4:26-34; Rom 14:17-21.
25. Cf. LG, n. 7; cf. 1 Cor 1:10-17; 3:3-9; 12:4-27; Eph 4:1-16; Col 3:12-17.
26. Cf. LG, n. 6; CCC, n. 753-757.
27. Cf. Ex 19:5-6; Deut 7:6; Mic 4:1-4.
28. Cf. Rom 12:3-21; 1 Cor 12:12-31.
29. Cf. Jn 10:1-16; Ezek 34:11-31.
30. Cf. Mt 21:33-43; Jn 15:1-11.
31. Cf. 1 Cor 3:5-23; Eph 2:19-22; 1 Pet 2:1-9.
32. Cf. Rev 21:1-27; Col 3:1-17.
33. Cf. Mt 22:1-14; 2 Cor 11:2.
34. Cf. Mt 12:46-50; Eph 2:19.

Witnesses to the
Word of God

19. The Word of God comes to us both through sacred Scripture and through the living witness of the Church, including men and women who have carefully and devoutly listened to the Word of God, have faithfully lived it and courageously given witness to it. Growing communion among Christians can only flow from following Jesus, the Word of God made flesh. The Virgin Mary, the saints and the martyrs in all ages of history have inspired and sustained Christians in walking as Christ's disciples.

Christ, the Faithful Witness

20. *"Grace to you and peace from him who is and who was and who is to come ... and from Jesus Christ, the faithful witness, the firstborn of the dead."*[35] Christ's whole earthly life — his words and deeds, his silence and suffering — is the revelation of the Father. Jesus says: *"Whoever has seen me has seen the Father,"*[36] and the Father says, *"This is my Son, my Chosen; listen to him!"*[37] The Word who became flesh is our model of holiness: *"Take my yoke upon*

---

35. Rev 1:4-5.
36. Jn 14:9.
37. Lk 9:35.

you, and learn from me";[38] *"Love one another as I have loved you."*[39]

The mystery of unity stands at the very heart of Christ's life and mission. The Spirit therefore calls all the faithful to place themselves before Christ and to learn from him how to forge bonds of communion in true discipleship. Only when keeping their eyes on Christ and listening to him will they find the light and the strength needed to continue the long and arduous pilgrimage of unity.

21. The reconciling power of the Gospel can be seen and heard throughout Christ's entire life, in many moments that illustrate and make effective his prayer that *"all may be one"*:

- his proclamation of the Beatitudes, as a new way of life ordered to the Kingdom of Heaven;[40]
- his preferential love for the sick, the needy and the poor, calling them from the margins of social and religious life to the very center of the new community he establishes;
- the primacy of love which *"binds everything together in perfect harmony"*;[41] this includes

---

38. Mt 11:29.
39. Jn 15:12.
40. Mt 5:3-12.
41. Col 3:14.

his teaching on not judging others,[42] on forgiving one another as God in Christ has forgiven us,[43] without limit and measure, as many as *"seventy times seven times"*;[44] with a love that extends even to our enemies;[45]

- his teaching about the Kingdom and about the relations which should prevail among his disciples, relations based on humble service and self-giving love;[46]

- his self-understanding as the Good Shepherd, who goes ahead of the sheep who *"follow him because they know his voice"* and who desires unity *"so there will be one flock, one shepherd"*;[47]

- his teaching about self-denial and taking up his Cross,[48] since *"he broke down the dividing wall of hostility … through the Cross, thereby bringing the hostility to an end"*;[49]

- his teaching about the Kingdom as a wedding banquet to which all are invited,[50] revealing God's desire to see the unity of all divided humanity restored and celebrated in Christ;

---

42. Cf. Mt 7:1-5.
43. Cf. Eph 4:32.
44. Cf. Mt 18:21-22.
45. Cf. Mt 5:43-48.
46. Cf. Mt 23:8-12; 20:20-28.
47. Jn 10:1-16.
48. Cf. Mt 16:24-28.
49. Eph 2:14-16.
50. Cf Mt 22:1-44.

- his prayer for his disciples and for all those who believe in him, that they might be one, a living communion;[51]
- his sacrifice on the Cross, giving his life for the unity of God's children, since *"Jesus would die for the nation, and not for the nation only, but to gather into one the dispersed children of God."*[52]

Together, Christians can

- pray that they may grow in true discipleship, following Jesus Christ, the "one shepherd";
- reflect upon the New Testament, so as to deepen their understanding of the Lord's reconciling ministry and to make it their own;
- rediscover common traditions stemming from the early Church and the centuries prior to the present divisions, notably writings or witnesses related to Jesus Christ;
- study theological and spiritual resources stemming from various traditions during the centuries of separation regarding the life and mission of Jesus Christ.

---

51. Cf Jn 17:1-26.
52. Jn 11:51-52.

Mary, the Mother of God

> *"Why should we not all together look to her as our*
> *common Mother, who prays for the unity of God's*
> *family and who 'precedes' us all at the head of the*
> *long line of witnesses of faith in the one Lord, the*
> *Son of God, who was conceived in her virginal*
> *womb by the power of the Holy Spirit?"*[53]

22. Mary, the Mother of God, has a particular place in the faith and spiritual life of the Church. According to sacred Scripture, Mary took part in a singular way in the Incarnation of the divine Word and in the Savior's work of redemption, by her obedience, faith, hope and burning charity.[54] Devotion to Mary, if rightly understood, does not obscure or diminish the unique mediation of Christ, but rather, shows its power and richness;[55] Christ is the one and only Mediator between God and humankind (1 Tim 2:5). What the Catholic Church believes about Mary is based on what it believes about Christ, and what it teaches about Mary in turn illumines its faith in Christ.[56]

Dying on the Cross, Christ entrusted his mother to the beloved disciple, with the words: *"Woman,*

53. Pope John Paul II, Encyclical Letter *Redemptoris Mater* (RM), n. 30.
54. Cf. LG, n. 60-65.
55. Cf. LG, n. 60; CCC, n. 2673-2679.
56. Cf. CCC, n. 487.

here is your son," and the disciple to his mother, saying *"Here is your mother"* (Jn 19:26-27).

23. Mary also accompanies the Church's journey toward Christian unity.[57] The Catholic Church and the Eastern Churches share the doctrine of the early Councils concerning the Virgin Mary, regarding Mary as *Theotókos,* Mother of God, and regarding her virginity;[58] they also share most liturgical celebrations of the Virgin Mary.[59] As to the Churches and Ecclesial Communities in the West, many of them hold the same doctrine of the early Councils regarding Mary and consider it as part of the one patrimony of faith; several liturgical celebrations of Mary are still on their liturgical calendars and are part of a common patrimony.[60] Some communities in the West, whose origins go back to pre-Reformation times, have kept Mary as their patron saint. Moreover, in many communities of the Reformation tradition, there is at present a renewed attentiveness to Mary as an "example of faith" and "our sister in faith." As to differences in doctrine and devotion, promising progress has been made toward a common understanding of the role of Mary in salvation history, thanks to the efforts of a number of

---

57. Cf. RM, n. 29-34.
58. Council of Ephesus (431): Denzinger-Schönmetzer, *Enchiridion Symbolorum* (DS) 251; Lateran Council of 649: DS 503; cf. DS 10-64.
59. Cf. UR, n. 15.
60. Particularly the Anglican Communion, the Scandinavian Lutheran Churches, the Old-Catholic Church.

ecumenical dialogues.[61] This progress touches issues which are mainly related to the dogmatic definitions of the second millennium and to some forms of popular devotion or religiosity. Though further dialogue may be required, the reception of these encouraging developments is one way of fostering spiritual ecumenism.

Together, Christians can

- acknowledge the place of Mary in sacred Scripture and ponder with her the great things that God has done in salvation history;
- study the witness of early Christianity regarding Mary, as reflected in liturgical celebrations, dogmatic definitions, prayers and devotions of the first centuries;
- promote mutual knowledge and appreciation of various traditions in devotion and spirituality related to the Mother of God in both the East and West;[62]
- pay due attention, in national or international sanctuaries dedicated to the Virgin Mary, to the presence and pastoral needs of those visitors who belong to other Churches and Ecclesial Communities, by making available appropriate prayers or

---

61. Cf. Bibliography: Ecumenical documents on Mary.
62. Cf. RM, n. 34.

meditations, along with the use of appropriate liturgical signs or symbols;[63]

- entrust prayers for the Church, particularly prayers for the unity of the Church, to the intercession of the Virgin Mary, whom many Christians venerate as Mother of the Church;[64] different forms of prayer to the Virgin Mary, such as the *Akathistos* hymn in the East and the prayer of the rosary in the West, can appropriately be recited as an intercession for the unity of all Christians.

Martyrs and Witnesses unto Death

"I have already remarked, and with deep joy, how an imperfect but real communion is preserved and is growing at many levels of ecclesial life. I now add that this communion is already perfect in what we all consider the highest point of the life of grace, martyria unto death, the truest communion possible with Christ who shed his Blood, and by that sacrifice brings near those who once were far off (cf. Eph 2:13)."[65]

---

63. Cf. Pontifical Council for the Pastoral Care of Migrants and Itinerant People, *The Shrine, Memory, Presence and Prophecy of the Living God*, 1999, n. 12.
64. Cf. CCC, n. 963-970.
65. UUS, n. 84.

24. The Church keeps the memorial of martyrs and commemorates those faithful who witnessed unto death, in all ages of Christian history. Even in recent times, under the brutal pressure of different ideologies or political regimes, numerous Christians of all traditions have suffered persecution and death for their fidelity to Christ and to the Church. Remembering them, Pope John Paul II asked that *"as far as possible, their witness should not be lost to the Church ... the local Churches should do everything possible to ensure that the memory of those who have suffered martyrdom should be safeguarded, gathering the necessary documentation. This gesture cannot fail to have an ecumenical character and expression. Perhaps the most convincing form of ecumenism is the ecumenism of the saints and of the martyrs. The communio sanctorum speaks louder than the things that divide us."*[66]

Together, Christians can

- offer ecumenical prayers for Christians of all traditions who still are victims of persecution and violence; the feast days of those martyrs whose names appear in liturgical calendars of various Churches and Ecclesial Communities provide an opportunity for such prayer (e.g., the feast of the beheading of Saint John the Baptist, the stoning of

---

66. Pope John Paul II, Apostolic Letter *Tertio Millennio Adveniente* (TMA), n. 37.

proto-martyr Saint Stephen, the martyrs of the first Christian centuries and later);

- publish locally or regionally updated registers and biographical notes regarding recent witnesses to the faith unto death; this can be done ecumenically, reminding everyone that the shedding of blood is a common inheritance of all Christian traditions;

- celebrate annually an *Ecumenical Commemoration of Witnesses to the Faith,* particularly in regions where the wounds of persecution and suffering still need healing; such a commemoration could take place during Lent or after Pentecost;[67]

- make use of prayers or meditations originating from different traditions which touch on the experience of martyrdom, when contemplating the passion and death of Jesus Christ and the Christian call to faithful witness.[68]

---

67. E.g. the *Ecumenical Commemoration of Witnesses to the Faith in the Twentieth Century,* presided over by Pope John Paul II on Sunday, May 7, 2000, at the Colosseum in Rome.
68. E.g., the Meditations for the Way of the Cross presided over by Pope John Paul II on Good Friday at the Colosseum in Rome, written by H.H. Bartholomew I, Ecumenical Patriarch of Constantinople (1994), Sister Minke de Vries from the community of Grandchamp (1995), H.H. Karekin I, Supreme Patriarch and Catholicos of All Armenians (1997) and Professor Olivier Clément of the Orthodox Church (1998).

Saints

> *"When we speak of a common heritage, we must acknowledge as part of it not only the institutions, rites, means of salvation and the traditions which all the communities have preserved and by which they have been shaped, but first and foremost this reality of holiness."*[69]

25. During the liturgical year, the Church commemorates and celebrates the saints of all ages, thanking God for the wonderful work of Christ in his servants and presenting their lives as fitting examples for imitation. The saints are also a source of hope in the quest for Christian unity. In various ways, holiness is a sign of Christ's victory over the divisive forces of sin and evil. Holiness of life is the first healing ointment, given by the Holy Spirit, to be applied on the wounds of disunity. During the history of the Church, saintly persons have been among the primary artisans of reconciliation and restored communion.

Together, Christians can

- draw attention to the common heritage of faith when commemorating saints of the apostolic period, such as the four Evangelists and the Apostles, whose names appear

---

69. UUS, n. 84.

in various liturgical calendars on the same day;

- give thanks to God for the saints of all ages who are remembered during the liturgical year in various Churches and Ecclesial Communities, for their holy witness or teaching that enriches the common Christian heritage. This includes saints who are traditionally celebrated in both East and West,[70] as well as those who are honoured by various Christian communities in the West;[71]

- celebrate the many saints who were particularly meritorious during their lifetimes in building bridges or promoting reconciliation among Christians; their liturgical commemoration can be given an ecumenical dimension;[72]

- commemorate ecumenically those local saints who were instrumental in the original spreading of the Gospel in a particular region, possibly by exchanging delegations or attending each other's worship;[73]

---

70. E.g. St. Athanasius the Great (+c.373), St. Cyril of Alexandria (+444), the Cappadocian Fathers: St. Basil of Cesarea (+379), St. Gregory of Nazianzus (+374), St. Gregory of Nyssa (+c.394).
71. E.g. St. Benedict of Norcia (+547), St. Francis of Assisi (+1226), St. Bridget of Sweden (+1373), Julian of Norwich (+1413).
72. E.g. St. Symeon Stylite (+459), St. Augustine of Canterbury (+604/609), St. John of Damascus (+c.754), St. Cyril (+869) and St. Methodius (+885).
73. E.g. the exchange of delegations between Rome and Constantinople on the Feast of St. Andrew in Constantinople (30 November) and on the Feast of Sts. Peter and Paul in Rome (29 June).

- acknowledge that the authentic relics and images of the saints are held in veneration, particularly though not exclusively in the Catholic and Orthodox tradition;[74] the translation or giving of relics of particular saints can become a significant moment of spiritual sharing;[75]
- draw from the sources of spiritual renewal found in the writings of spiritual masters whose lives and teachings are commonly considered as gifts of the Holy Spirit to the one Church of Christ.[76]

---

74. Cf. Second Vatican Council, Constitution on the Sacred Liturgy *Sacrosanctum Concilium* (SC), 1963, n. 111.
75. E.g. in 1968, Pope Paul VI gave relics of St. Mark to the Coptic Orthodox Church in Egypt; in 2000, Pope John Paul II gave relics of St. Gregory the Illuminator to the Catholicossate of All Armenians (Etchmiadzin) and in 2001 to the Catholicossate of Cilicia (Antelias); in 2004, Pope John Paul II gave relics of St. John Chrysostom and St. Gregory of Nazianzus to the Ecumenical Patriarchate of Constantinople.
76. E.g. Nil Sorskij (+1508), John Wesley (+1791), Seraphim of Sarov (+1833), Paul Wattson (+1940), Dietrich Bonhoeffer (+1945), Paul Couturier (+1953), Mary Elisabeth Hesselblad (+1957).

2
Prayer and Worship

The Lord's Prayer

26. *"Run through all the words of the holy prayers (in Scripture), and I do not think that you will find anything in them that is not contained and included in the Lord's Prayer."*[1] The Lord's Prayer is truly unique, in that it is "of the Lord" (Mt 6:9-13; Lk 11:2-4). The only Son gives us the words that the Father gave to him, and through the Spirit these words become in us "spirit and life."

The Lord's prayer opens with the profoundly intimate exclamation of "our Father." Together with the Lord, we give thanks to the Father for having revealed his name to us and for having adopted us as his children. Each of the baptized is praying "our Father" in communion with all who are baptized. For this reason, and in spite of divisions, the prayer of the "Our Father" remains a common patrimony of all Christians and an urgent summons to pray for their unity.[2]

In the first series of petitions, our hearts and minds turn toward God our Father, for his own sake: *"thy* name ... *thy* kingdom ... *thy* will...." Through these petitions, the Lord immerses us in the mystery of God's loving plan for the salvation of humanity. By contrast, division among Christians does not hallow the name of God, it does not hasten the coming of God's kingdom, nor does it

---

1. St. Augustine, Ep. 130, 12,22: PL 33,503; cf. CCC, n. 2759-2865.
2. Cf. CCC, n. 2791.

fulfill his will. When praying the Our Father,
Christians ask the Father insistently for his loving
plan to be fully realized on earth as it is in heaven;
this includes the healing of all divisions. They also
ask to discern together "what is the will of God"
and seek the strength to carry it out.[3]

In the second series, we present to God our
Father petitions that concern us: "give *us* ... forgive
us ... lead *us* not ... deliver *us*...." By praying the
"Our Father," Christians pray together that all
God's children may receive what is necessary for
life.[4] The drama of hunger in the world calls
Christians both to pray together and to exercise a
shared responsibility toward their brothers and
sisters in need.

The last petitions are about sinfulness and
forgiveness. Though clothed with the baptismal
garment, Christians continue to struggle with
the sin of disunity. Dissension and discord are
among the ever present temptations. Without
examination of conscience, repentance, conversion and absolute trust in the reconciling power
of God's love, there is no journey toward Christian unity. Praying to be delivered from the Evil
One, Christians implore the precious gift of peace
and unity and the grace of perseverance in a
shared expectation of Christ's return in glory.

---

3. Cf. Rom 12:2.
4. Cf. 1 Tim 6:8.

Personal Prayer

"As the Church turns her gaze to the new millennium, she asks the Spirit for the grace to strengthen her own unity and to make it grow toward full communion with other Christians. How is the Church to obtain this grace? In the first place, through prayer. Prayer should always concern itself with the longing for unity, and as such is one of the basic forms of our love for Christ and for the Father who is rich in mercy. In this journey which we are undertaking with other Christians ... prayer must occupy the first place."[5]

27. Jesus prayed to his Father for the gift of unity. From that time on, the Church unites itself with Christ beseeching the Father, praying for the unity that Christ desires in the way he desires it.[6] Thus prayer for unity remains at the heart of any Christian prayer.[7]

In their personal prayer, Christians can

- give due attention to prayer for unity in the celebration of the Eucharist;
- insert, where possible, particular intercessions for Christian unity in the liturgical

5. UUS, n. 102.
6. This expression of Fr. Paul Couturier has since 1938 become a *leitmotif* for the annual Week of Prayer for Christian Unity.
7. Cf. UUS, n. 27.

prayer of the Church (Liturgy of the Hours, Office of Readings);

- offer daily prayer or devotions for the intention of Christian unity (e.g., the Rosary, Eucharistic Adoration);
- seek Christian unity through fasting, penance and personal conversion;
- unite their hardship and suffering with Christ for the intention of Christian unity.

Prayer in Common

"In certain special circumstances, such as the prescribed prayers 'for unity,' and during ecumenical gatherings, it is allowable and indeed desirable that Catholics should join in prayer with other Christians. Such prayers in common are certainly an effective means of obtaining the grace of unity, and they are a true expression of the ties which still bind Catholics to their separated fellow Christians: 'for where two or three are gathered together in my name, there am I in the midst of them' (Mt 18:20)."[8]

28. Christians are encouraged to join in prayer with members of other Churches and Ecclesial Communities. Prayer in common is an effective means of petitioning God for the fullness of Christian unity, and gives genuine expression to the deep bond that exists between them. Prayer for the restoration of unity should therefore find a prominent place in any prayer in common. Such prayer might focus on the mystery of the Church and its unity, on Baptism as a sacramental bond of unity, on the renewal of personal and communal life, or on the healing of the brokenness of humanity.[9]

---

8. UR, n. 8.
9. Cf. Directory, n. 110.

The celebration of the annual Week of Prayer for Christian Unity world-wide is an initiative of singular importance to be encouraged and further developed.[10]

29. Christians can benefit from taking part in liturgical services and non-sacramental celebrations of other communities. Such participation is an opportunity to better understand each other's communal prayer and to share more deeply in liturgical traditions which often have developed from common roots.[11] Since liturgical traditions are part of the sacred heritage of Churches and Ecclesial Communities and are constitutive of their identity, sharing liturgical worship requires a meticulous regard for the sensibilities of all those concerned, as well as for particular customs which may vary according to time, place, persons and circumstances.[12] Rather than blending liturgical elements stemming from various traditions, in ecumenical prayer preference should be given to preserving the particularity of existing forms of liturgical worship. Such a regard for the authentic diversity within our traditions gives better expression to the unity in diversity for which we are striving.

---

10. Every year the World Council of Churches (Geneva) and the Pontifical Council for Promoting Christian Unity (Vatican) seek the assistance of a local community in preparing the materials for the Week of Prayer.
11. Cf. Directory, n. 117.
12. Cf. Directory, n. 119.

30. In many parts of the world, Christians also join in ecumenical prayer services which mark important events related to local history, civil society or social life. In some countries major events for the nation or for civil society are often commemorated with ecumenical worship.[13] These ecumenical prayer services give voice to the shared concerns and hopes of Christians in that region and are an eloquent means of common witness.

Christians can pray together:

- during the annual Week of Prayer for Christian Unity (18 to 25 January or another appropriate time, often the period between Ascension and Pentecost);[14]
- on the occasion of ecumenical gatherings;
- during some important periods of the liturgical year (e.g., Advent, Christmas, Lent and Easter) and in conjunction with major feasts;
- in remembrance of the dead, or those who died for their country;
- in times of public disaster or mourning;
- on significant days in the life of other Churches and Ecclesial Communities (like Sunday of Orthodoxy, Reformation Day);
- amidst situations of profound human need, and in response to shared concerns (e.g., for peace and justice in the world, the allevia-

13. Cf. Directory, n. 109.
14. Cf. Directory, n. 110.

tion of poverty, hunger and violence; for respecting the dignity of the family);

- when a nation, region or community collectively gives thanks or intercedes before God;

- on the occasion of world-wide days of prayer for particular groups or intentions (e.g. World Youth Days);

- on particular days in public or social life (e.g. New Year's Day, the beginning or end of a school year, the beginning or end of holidays, thanksgiving for the fruits of the earth).

31. "No one can say 'Jesus is Lord,' except by the Holy Spirit" (1 Cor 12:3). Whenever Christians gather to pray, it is the Holy Spirit who moves them and teaches them to pray. The Holy Spirit is also the source of Christian unity, since "it is the Holy Spirit, dwelling in those who believe and pervading and ruling over the entire Church, who brings about that wonderful communion of the faithful and joins them together so intimately in Christ that he is the principle of the Church's unity.[15] Many Christians of various traditions today have testified to a profound experience of the presence of the Holy Spirit. As a result, prayer in the Holy Spirit is for them a source of personal renewal and of deeper belonging

---

15. UR, n. 2.

to the Body of Christ. Calling upon the Holy Spirit, they grow closer to Jesus Christ and to another. The criteria for discerning the authenticity of the working of the Holy Spirit, given by Saint Paul[16] and further developed in the spiritual tradition of the Church, are a help and a norm for them and for all Christians. Attentive to these criteria, living a life of discipleship and prayer receptive to the Holy Spirit can become a true means of mutual edification and can deepen the bonds of communion among Christians.

---

16. Cf. 1 Cor 12-14; Gal 5:22-26.

Sacramental Celebrations

32. Sacraments are salvific actions of Jesus Christ, through the ministry of the Church. They are carried out in the power of the Holy Spirit to the glory of the Father. By their celebration, they draw the faithful to participate even now in God's life.[17] The sacraments are an expression of the Church's unity in faith, in worship and in apostolic ministry; they are also a source of the Church's unity and a means for building it up. For this reason, sacramental celebrations, particularly the Eucharist, are essentially related to full ecclesial communion and its visible expression.[18] Since sacramental celebrations are among the most important actions of the Church, belonging in varying ways and degrees to all Christian traditions, they too have their place in spiritual ecumenism.

---

17. Cf. CCC, n. 1113-1116.
18. Cf. Directory, n. 129.

Baptism

> *"Baptism establishes a sacramental bond of unity existing among all who have been reborn by it. But of itself baptism is only a beginning, an inauguration wholly directed toward the acquisition of the fullness of life in Christ. Baptism, therefore, is oriented toward the complete profession of faith, complete incorporation into the institution of salvation such as Christ willed it to be, and finally the completeness of unity which eucharistic communion gives."[19]*

33. Baptism is the primary sacrament of salvation, through which people become Christians, incorporated into Christ and into his Church.[20] In terms of Christian unity, it is the sacrament which constitutes the foundation of communion among all Christians. That is why there are important possibilities for spiritual ecumenism in connection with this sacrament. When Christians rediscover together the mystery and the spiritual riches of their baptism, they grow closer to Jesus Christ and to one another; they become more aware of their belonging to the one Body of Christ and of their common vocation. The recognition of each other's baptism allows the possibility of gathering in celebrations which affirm or commemorate the grace of baptism; such gatherings have been

19. Cf. UR, n. 22.
20. Cf. 1 Cor 12:13; Gal 3:28.

introduced in some parts of the world.[21] Joining in thanksgiving and intercession, they express gratitude to the Lord for the gift of salvation through baptism, asking that together they may grow toward the fullness of unity.

An ecumenical affirmation or commemoration of baptism can

- be celebrated where Christians of various Churches and Ecclesial Communities are living and working together;
- be a way of marking significant days or seasons during the liturgical year (e.g. Baptism of the Lord, season of Easter and Pentecost);
- be a welcome occasion for a common catechesis on the mystery and the effects of baptism.[22]

34. Unity in Christ is, first of all, unity in the faith of the Church and in the confession of faith, made during baptism. Christians profess "one Lord, one faith, one baptism" (Eph 4:5). The faith of the Church has been expressed in the early Creeds, particularly in the Apostles' Creed which is the ancient baptismal symbol of the Church of Rome and in the Nicene-Constantinopolitan Creed which stems from the first two ecumenical Councils, that of Nicea (325 A.D.) and that of

---

21. Cf. Directory, n. 96.
22. Cf. Bibliography: Ecumenical documents on the sacraments.

Constantinople (381 A.D.). The elements of faith found in these Creeds remain common to the great Churches and Ecclesial Communities of both East and West, even if not always professed by the same formulation.[23] The "articles of faith" therefore are a sign of recognition and communion between believers,[24] and a "standard of teaching" which allows them to grow closer to one another. Using the Creed to profess their faith, Christians enter into communion with God — Father, Son and Holy Spirit — and also with the whole Church.[25]

Together, Christians can

- promote shared formation programs to deepen their understanding of Christian faith, "the faith of our baptism";
- study together authoritative teaching documents from their respective traditions, regarding questions of faith;
- study and reflect together upon the results of ecumenical dialogues through which questions regarding the doctrine of faith have been clarified.[26]

---

23. Cf. CCC, n. 195; CCC Compendium, question 35.
24. Cf. CCC, n. 188.
25. Cf. CCC, n. 197.
26. Cf. Bibliography: Ecumenical documents on matters of faith.

Eucharist

> *"The cup of blessing which we bless, is it not a participation in the blood of Christ? The bread that we break, is it not a participation in the body of Christ? Because there is one bread, we who are many are one body, for we all partake of the one bread" (1 Cor 10:16-17).*

35. Through their baptism, Christians are called to form one body in Jesus Christ;[27] in the Eucharist, this call to unity with God and with each other is brought to fulfillment. Therefore, *"truly partaking of the body of the Lord in the breaking of the Eucharistic bread, we are taken up into communion with Him and with one another.... In this way all of us are made members of His Body (cf. 1 Cor 12:27) 'but severally members one of another' (Rom 12:5)."*[28]

36. Since earliest times, the celebration of the Eucharist has included several prayers for reconciliation and for the unity of the Church: *as this broken bread, once spread over the hills, was brought together and became one loaf, so may your Church be brought together from the ends of the earth into your Kingdom.*[29] During the Eucharistic Prayer or Anaphora, the Latin tradition prays that *"all of us who share in the body and blood of Christ may be*

---

27. Cf. 1 Cor 12:13.
28. LG n. 7; cf. also SC, n. 48; LG, n. 3; 11; 26.
29. *Didache* 9,4, from the second century.

brought together in unity by the Holy Spirit";[30] the Eastern tradition prays that *"God may put an end to the schisms of the Churches, stop the arrogance of the nations, repel the appearance of heresies, through the power of the Holy Spirit. Receive us all in your Kingdom and make us children of light and day. Grant us your peace and your love, God our Lord, You who has given us everything.*[31] In catechesis and liturgical formation it is appropriate to give due attention to the gift of unity, which the Church prays for and receives in every eucharistic celebration.

The Eucharist is the privileged place to pray for unity:

- as a memorial of the Paschal mystery of the Cross and Resurrection of Jesus Christ, every Eucharist celebrates atonement, reconciliation, integrity and unity; it is therefore appropriate that these themes are addressed in the proclamation of the Word, which needs to relate the scriptural readings and prayers to this core mystery of our salvation;

- since the Missal of the Latin tradition provides votive masses for the intention of Christian unity, these can be celebrated not only during the annual Week of Prayer for

---

30. Eucharistic Prayer II.
31. Anaphora of the Liturgy of St. Basil.

Christian Unity, but also on other occasions during the liturgical year;[32]

- during the Eucharist, intercessions for unity can be inserted in the prayers of the faithful or in the prayers known as *"Ectenie"* litanies in the Eastern liturgy;[33]

- as each liturgical feast or season draws attention to certain dimensions of the mystery of salvation, in the Eucharistic celebration different aspects of the search for unity come to light: Advent (a longing for the unity which only God can give), Christmas (the Word became flesh to unite all things in God), Lent (unity related to conversion or forgiveness), Easter (unity in the one Risen Lord and in one Baptism), Pentecost (unity and the gifts of the Holy Spirit), All Saints (unity in holiness or martyrdom).

37. Eucharistic and ecclesial communion are intrinsically linked to one another. Therefore, as long as fundamental disagreements in matters of faith persist and the bonds of communion are not fully re-established, celebrating together the one Eucharist of the Lord is not possible. Fortunately, through ecumenical dialogue, significant progress has been made toward a common understanding of constitutive elements of faith, including the

---

32. Cf. Directory, n. 62.
33. Ibid.

true meaning of the Lord's Supper.[34] Though the full consensus which would allow a common celebration of the Eucharist has not yet been reached, these ecumenical developments hold the promise of further convergence and deserve greater attention.[35]

38. As to the practice of sharing in sacramental life with members of other Churches and Ecclesial Communities, the Second Vatican Council laid down two basic principles that belong together: *"first, the bearing witness to the unity of the Church, and second, the sharing in the means of grace. Witness to the unity of the Church generally forbids common worship, but the grace to be had from it sometimes commends this practice.*[36] In the light of these two basic principles, the Catholic Church does not allow sharing the Eucharist until the visible bonds of ecclesial communion are fully re-established, though in certain circumstances and under certain conditions it permits Catholic ministers to give Holy Communion to other Christians, under the authority of the local bishop. More specifically, Catholic ministers may give Holy Communion to members of the Eastern Churches whenever they ask for it of their own will and possess the required dispositions; they may give Holy Communion to members of other ecclesial communities if, in grave necessity,

34. Cf. UR, n. 15 (Eastern Churches) and UR, n. 22 (Churches and Ecclesial Communities in the West).
35. Cf. Bibliography: Ecumenical documents on the sacraments.
36. Cf. UR, n. 8.

they ask for it of their own will, possess the required dispositions, and give evidence of holding the Catholic faith regarding the sacrament.[37] Conversely the Catholic Church allows its members in certain circumstances and under certain conditions to receive Holy Communion from ministers of Churches where a valid Eucharist is celebrated. These provisions have been laid down in specific guidelines and norms, which reflect the present state of division and growing communion between the Catholic Church and other Churches and Ecclesial Communities.[38] Respecting carefully these norms is an appropriate way of honoring the sacrament of the Eucharist and furthering the search for unity.

---

37. Cf. CCC, Compendium, question 293.
38. Cf. UR, n. 8 and 15; OE, n. 26-29; CIC, can. 844; CCEO, can. 671; Directory, n. 122-128 and 129-136; UUS, n. 46; Pope John Paul II, Encyclical Letter *Ecclesia de Eucharistia*, 2003 (EDE) n. 43-46; CCC, n. 1398-1401.

Mixed Marriage Families

> *"Marriages between Catholics and other baptized persons have their own particular nature, but they contain numerous elements that could well be made good use of and developed, both for their intrinsic value and for the contribution that they can make to the ecumenical movement. This is particularly true when both parties are faithful to their religious duties. Their common Baptism and the dynamism of grace provide the spouses in these marriages with the basis and motivation for expressing their unity in the sphere of moral and spiritual values."* [39]

39. Mixed marriage families are an ever present reality in many parts of the world. While not turning a blind eye to the challenges faced by mixed marriage couples, the Catholic Church looks to them also in terms of their intrinsic value and invites reflection on the contributions they can make to their respective communities, as they live out their Christian discipleship faithfully and creatively. [40] Mixed marriage families have indeed something to offer in terms of an ecumenical exchange of gifts.

40. Pastoral guidelines and norms have been laid down by the Church regarding the preparation and celebration of mixed marriages, the

---

39. Pope John Paul II, Encyclical Letter *Familiaris Consortio*, n. 78.
40. Cf. CCC, n. 1633-1637.

sharing in sacramental life, the responsibilities of
parents for the upbringing of the children, and
the responsibilities of the local Ordinary and
ministers, responding to the pastoral needs of
mixed marriage families.[41] Faithfulness to these
guidelines and norms will at times mean that
mixed marriage families will feel intensely
the pain of division between the communities
to which they belong. That same faithfulness,
however, will also help them to take part more
fully and personally in the quest for restored
communion between these communities. The
particular experiences of mixed marriage families
should be given due pastoral consideration both
in terms of the gifts and the challenges they bring
to their communities.

In the local Church, mixed marriage families
can

- be encouraged, as a couple or family, to
  pray and to ponder the Scriptures, as a way
  of nourishing their spiritual life;[42]
- be ministered to by dioceses or local communities, particularly in the period of marriage
  preparation, through programs which help
  these couples to better understand each

41. CIC, can. 1124-1129; CCEO, can. 813-816; Directory, n. 143-160.
42. Cf. Directory, n. 149.

partner's religious convictions and deepen their shared Christian inheritance;[43]

- be called upon to play a role in organizing or leading ecumenical groups who gather for prayer and the study of Scriptures, or for the support of other mixed marriage families;
- be given a particular responsibility in the preparation of ecumenical prayer services, both during the Week of Prayer for Christian Unity and throughout the year;
- be invited to study and make known the Church's teaching concerning the promotion of Christian unity and developments resulting from ecumenical dialogue.

---

43. Cf. Directory, n. 149; cf. Bibliography: Ecumenical documents on the sacraments.

Sacraments of Healing

41. Through Baptism Christians are incorporated into Christ and into his Body, the Church. This bond of unity, however, has been deeply wounded by the divisive effects of human sinfulness. In any serious commitment to Christian unity, therefore, the Spirit calls Christians to place themselves before God, to recognize their own faults, to confess their sins and ask forgiveness, entrusting themselves into the hands of the One who is our Intercessor before the Father, Jesus Christ.[44] The sacrament of Penance/Reconciliation repairs the breaches caused by sin and restores our wounded communion with God and with the Church. The sacrament of the Anointing of the Sick brings healing to the seriously ill and the dying, binding them more closely to God and to their brothers and sisters in Christ.

In certain circumstances and under certain conditions, which are the same as those mentioned above regarding the Eucharist, Catholic ministers may give the sacraments of Penance/Reconciliation and Anointing of the Sick to members of other Churches and Ecclesial Communities; conversely Catholics under certain conditions can request these same sacraments from minis-

---

44. Cf. UUS, n. 82.

ters of Churches in which these sacraments are valid.[45]

Together, Christians can

- gather in particular seasons of the liturgical year, such as Lent, for a common service based on biblical readings on forgiveness and mercy, in preparation for approaching a minister of one's own Church for personal confession of sins and absolution;
- work together in chaplaincy and pastoral care in locations such as hospitals, prisons or refugee camps, bringing the healing power of Christ to those in need.[46]

45. Cf. UR, n. 8 and 15; OE, n. 26-29; CIC, can. 844; CCEO, can. 671; Directory, n. 122-128 and 129-136.
46. Cf. Directory, n. 204.

The Liturgical Year

42. The whole history and economy of salvation is celebrated and made present in the span of a liturgical year. Though following the same basic pattern, ecclesial traditions in East and West gave different shape to the liturgical calendar. They all celebrate the Paschal mystery as the central event of salvation history, with Easter as the annual and Sunday as a weekly commemoration of the Lord's death and resurrection.[47] All liturgical celebrations, including feasts of saints and martyrs, revolve around the central mystery of Christ's redeeming work. The liturgical year, also called the "year of the Lord" or the "year of Grace," is the recurring joint pilgrimage of all Christians.

43. Through its successive seasons and celebrations, the liturgical year molds and fashions Christian faithful and communities, enabling them to grow in faith and love. Spiritual ecumenism finds its proper place within this framework. Many liturgical seasons or feasts offer favorable opportunities for developing themes of Christian unity and for shared study, reflection or prayer.[48] In some parts of the world, an annual ecumenical calendar already exists, indicating

---

47. Continuous efforts should therefore be made to find a common date in the Christian East and West for the celebration of Easter; cf. SC, *Addendum, Declaration of the Most Sacred Second Council of the Vatican on Revision of the Calendar.*
48. Cf. Directory, n. 60.

various moments which are particularly apt for a sharing in spiritual activities.

44. Though there is no liturgical calendar common to all Christian Churches and communities, the principal Christian feasts (such as Christmas, Epiphany, Easter and Pentecost) follow a similar sequence in all traditions. While the outline below presents examples for joint ecumenical initiatives according to the calendar of the Latin tradition in the Catholic Church, those Christians following a different liturgical calendar may also find them helpful.

Advent and Christmas:

- Advent: Vespers with reflection or preaching; Advent worship with Scripture readings and hymns; ecumenical prayer for families;
- December 24th afternoon: celebration with children focusing on the Nativity scene or re-enacting the Christmas story;
- Christmas season: Vespers or "Songs of Praise" with local or traditional Christmas carols;
- December 31st: common prayer service of thanksgiving and intercession;
- Epiphany: the practice in some countries of children visiting houses singing Christmas and Epiphany carols can be organized ecumenically.

Lent and Holy Week:

- Ash Wednesday or beginning of Lent: Vespers or common prayer service, encouraging Christians to embrace together the traditional Lenten practices of prayer, fasting and almsgiving;
- Evenings in Lent: study series on an ecumenical topic;
- Weekdays in Lent: solidarity meeting or meal focusing attention on a common concern or offering support for people in a specific region;
- Friday before Palm Sunday or during Holy Week: public Way of the Cross, particularly for young people; prayer, meditations, traditional hymns on the Passion of Jesus Christ.

Easter till Pentecost:

- Easter season: Vespers with exchange of Easter candles between neighboring communities; "Songs of Praise" with traditional Easter hymns;
- Easter Monday: shared reflections on the Gospel reading of the disciples on the road to Emmaus;
- Ascension to Pentecost (Pentecost Novena): Week of Prayer for Christian Unity;
- Pentecost season: Liturgy of the Word with ecumenical commemoration of Baptism;

Vespers with preaching and meditation on the Holy Spirit; "Songs of Praise" with traditional hymns to the Holy Spirit.

During the year, according to local customs and seasons:

- Beginning of January: common prayer service for peace;
- January 18-25: Week of Prayer for Christian Unity;
- End of January: Bible-Sunday for various age or social groups;
- Sunday of Orthodoxy (first Sunday of Lent in the Orthodox Churches): prayer for the Orthodox Churches and for the restoration of unity between East and West;
- Spring or early Summer: outdoor celebration in thanksgiving for creation and nature;
- Last days of school year: liturgy of the Word with thanksgiving for the blessing of the past year and prayer for the forthcoming holidays;
- Summer holidays: ecumenical pilgrimages, Bible camps for young people;
- Beginning of new school year: celebration for students and teachers, asking God's blessing on the forthcoming academic year;
- Harvest Season: festival of the "fruits of the earth" expressing gratitude and praise to the Creator;

- Reformation Day: prayer for the restoration of unity between the Catholic Church and the Churches and Ecclesial Communities in the Reformation tradition;
- November 1st, All Saints: Vespers with preaching or meditation on the common Christian vocation to holiness;
- November 2nd, All Souls: Vespers with preaching or meditation in commemoration of those who have died in the various local Churches and Ecclesial Communities;
- Days focusing on world development: prayer services centering on issues of justice, peace and the integrity of creation;
- Annual day of penance and prayer: ecumenical worship focusing on conversion and unity;
- In times of conflict, disaster or war: common prayer, fasting and almsgiving.

3
"Diakonia"
and Witness

Parishes and
Local Communities

"To make the Church the home and the school of communion: that is the great challenge facing us in the millennium which is now beginning, if we wish to be faithful to God's plan and respond to the world's deepest yearnings."[1]

45. Division is most visible and tangible where people of diverse Churches and Ecclesial Communities live side by side in cities and villages. In some places, the effects of division are deeply ingrained in the collective consciousness and memory of a populace, often giving rise to parallel and rival structures of social and ecclesial life. It is there that parishes and local communities have a special responsibility to be artisans of reconciliation, fostering growth in communion. They can be encouraged to do so in various ways.

46. First, Christians can witness to genuine unity in diversity by building a community that is peaceful within itself, and that is not torn apart by internal polemics, ideological polarization or mutual recrimination.[2]

---

1. Pope John Paul II, Apostolic Letter *Novo Millennio Ineunte* (NMI), n. 43.
2. Cf. Directory, n. 67.

Wherever Christians live or work together, they can be encouraged

- to meet in their neighborhoods to deepen everyday relations of friendship, particularly among families;
- to foster relations of cooperation and shared commitment in the workplace, and to jointly address work-related or social issues;
- to express the values of their own traditions, keeping faithful to them without denigrating others or engaging in polemics;
- to avoid attitudes, gestures or actions that may hurt the feelings of Christians belonging to other traditions;
- to be generous or open in day-to-day relations with other Christians, trying to overcome inappropriate expressions of present divisions.

47. Second, effective channels of communication and cooperation between parishes and local communities can be cultivated through regular contact between their respective pastoral ministers, together with those having responsibility for particular aspects of the local community's life and mission.

Together, local communities and their leaders can

- forward information to each other about major events, particular celebrations, specific programs;
- communicate information among themselves through bulletins, press releases or circular letters;
- exchange delegations or messages on particular occasions (e.g., ordinations, consecrations, funerals);
- set up or support a local Council of Churches *"to enable their members to work together, to engage in dialogue, to overcome divisions and misunderstandings, to engage in prayer and work for unity, and to give, as far as possible, a common Christian witness and service"*;[3]
- facilitate and support ministerial associations or regular meetings between local pastoral ministers.

48. Third, parishes and local communities have a responsibility to work together in responding to the needs of the contemporary world, seeking to do everything together that is allowed by their faith.[4] Instead of working in isolation from one another, they can participate in existing programs set up by one of the local

---

3. Cf. Directory, n. 166.
4. Cf. Directory, n. 162.

Churches or Ecclesial Communities, take part in joint initiatives, and strive to coordinate their social efforts, thus avoiding duplication or unnecessary multiplication of administrative structures.[5] This ecumenical cooperation is of vital importance not only for greater effectiveness, but also for the sake of common witness and spiritual ecumenism. It gives tangible expression to the bond that already unites them and to their shared discipleship in following Christ the Servant (cf. Mk 10:45; Phil 2:5-8).[6]

Christian communities can develop common initiatives

- in catechesis and continuing formation;[7]
- in pastoral care of particular groups of people, such as those who are in hospitals, prisions, the armed forces and universities;[8]
- in mission to those who have never heard the Gospel of Jesus Christ and in evangelization of those whose faith is challenged by contemporary secular society;[9]
- in promoting the dignity of the human person;
- in the application of Gospel principles to social and cultural life;

---

5. Cf. Directory, n. 163.
6. Cf. UR., n. 12; cf. Bibliography: Ecumenical documents on mission and common witness.
7. Cf. Directory, n. 188.
8. Cf. Directory, n. 204.
9. Cf. Directory, n. 205-209.

- in the use of every possible means to relieve those suffering from famine and natural disasters, illiteracy and poverty, lack of housing and the unequal distribution of wealth;[10]
- in producing or promoting joint programs on radio, television, internet and other media;[11]
- in engaging together in interreligious dialogue, especially given its increasing importance in many parts of the world.[12]

---

10. Cf. UR, n. 12; *Directory*, n. 211-216; local communities can also assist such efforts through international aid or relief agencies such as *Caritas International* with its members and partners, which often work ecumenically in addressing situations of crisis or profound need.
11. Cf. *Directory*, n. 217-218.
12. Cf. *Directory*, n. 210.

Communities
of Religious Life

"Since the soul of ecumenism is prayer and conversion, Institutes of Consecrated Life and Societies of Apostolic Life certainly have a special duty to foster this commitment. There is an urgent need for consecrated persons to give more space in their lives to ecumenical prayer and genuine evangelical witness, so that by the power of the Holy Spirit the walls of division and prejudice between Christians can be broken down."[13]

49. In their rich variety of spiritual traditions and pastoral activities, Institutes of Consecrated Life and Societies of Apostolic Life are a gift of the Holy Spirit to the Church. Their contribution to the promotion of spiritual ecumenism is intrinsically related to their radical commitment to the Gospel, through fidelity to the evangelical counsels and their manifold apostolic activities in the Church and in the world.[14] Since consecrated life has at its heart "the following of Christ as proposed by the Gospel,"[15] it also embodies the Lord's yearning *"that all may be one"* (Jn 17:21).

---

13. Pope John Paul II, Apostolic Exhortation *Vita Consecrata* (VC), n. 100.
14. Cf. Directory, n. 50 a.
15. Second Vatican Council, Decree on the Sensitive Renewal of Religious Life *Perfectae Caritatis*, 1965, n. 2.

Through the course of history, many religious founders and foundresses, under the inspiration of the Holy Spirit, have made significant contributions to a deepening of Christian spirituality and to the search for unity. Their example and teaching, though originally rooted in particular times and places, remain a source of inspiration for all Christians.

Religious communities can

- foster spiritual ecumenism by making available to all Christians the spiritual treasures entrusted to them, such as the writings or teachings of their founders and foundresses;[16]
- offer their resources to host and facilitate ecumenical gatherings for prayer, for retreats or spiritual exercises, and for conferences of various kinds; this enables them also to share their spiritual traditions with ecumenical guests;[17]
- develop relations between communities of different traditions, leading to an exchange

---

16. E.g., the lives and teachings of St. Basil of Cesarea (+379), St. Augustine of Hippo (+430), St. Francis (+1226) and St. Clare (+1253) of Assisi, St. Dominic (+1221), St. Ignatius of Loyola (+1556), St. Teresa of Avila (+1582), Blessed Charles de Foucauld (+1916), Blessed Mother Teresa of Calcutta (+1997).
17. Cf. Directory, 50 c.

of spiritual and intellectual resources and a sharing of experiences in apostolic life;[18]

- take seriously the ecumenical potential of schools, hospitals and other apostolates, such that each and every Christian receives appropriate spiritual assistance in accordance with his or her own tradition and needs.

18. Cf. Directory, 50 d.

Monastic Communities

50. Monastic communities have a vocation to seek God through a common life centered on prayer, sacrifice and service. Throughout the centuries they have been instrumental in helping Christians of different traditions to grow closer to Jesus Christ and to one another. Monastic spirituality, which first flourished in the East, has been a significant bridge between Christians in the East and in the West.[19] In recent times, some communities of monastic life have been founded with an explicitly ecumenical commitment; spiritual ecumenism touches the heart of their charism and daily life.[20] Other communities, founded in more than one Church or Ecclesial Community, share deep bonds arising from the fact that they are rooted in the same spiritual tradition.[21] These communities have unique opportunities for encounter and mutual enrichment among Christians of different traditions sharing a common spiritual journey.

---

19. Cf. UR, n. 15; VC, n. 101; Pope John Paul II, Apostolic Letter *Orientale Lumen* (OL), n. 9-16.
20. Cf. VC, n. 101; e.g., the Monastery of Chevetogne, the Community of Taizé, the Community of Grandchamp, the Monastic Community of Bose.
21. E.g. monastic communities, both Catholic and Orthodox, living according to the tradition of St. Basil; religious communities living according to the rule of St. Benedict or the rule of St. Francis, both in the Catholic Church and in the Anglican Communion.

Monastic communities can

- be centers of prayer and self-giving for the cause of Christian unity (e.g., the life of Maria Gabriella of Unity,+1939);
- offer hospitality and bring together Christians of various traditions in a spiritual family that extends beyond the bounds of the monastery, creating a *milieu* for friendship and ecumenical exchange;
- organize exchanges or visits with other monasteries so as to allow their members to become acquainted with the particularities and riches of different traditions (e.g., Coptic, Ethiopian, Syrian, Armenian, Greek, Slavonic and Latin monastic traditions);
- promote joint studies and publications on the major figures of monasticism in both East and West, and on their spiritual teaching.[22]

---

22. E.g., the lives and writings of St. Anthony the Great (+356), St. Pachomius (+346/347), Evagrius Ponticus (+399), St. John Cassian (+432/435), St. Benedict of Norcia (+547), St. Isaac of Niniveh (+end 7th.), Gregory of Narek (+c.1003), Simeon the New Theologian (+1022), St. Bernard of Clairvaux (+1153), St. John of the Cross (+1591), St. Thérèse (of the Child Jesus) of Lisieux (+1897), Blessed Elizabeth of the Trinity (+1906), Silvanos of Mount Athos (+1938).

Ecclesial Communities
or Movements

"Those involved in such groups, movements and associations should be imbued with a solid ecumenical spirit, in living their baptismal commitment in the world, whether by seeking Catholic unity through dialogue and communion with similar movements and associations — or the wider communion with other Churches and Ecclesial Communities and with the movements and groups inspired by them."[23]

51. Many communities, movements or associations of the faithful have been founded, particularly in recent times, each with a specific charism;[24] some have a particular vocation to promote Christian unity and spiritual ecumenism. A common characteristic of these movements is that they invite their members to live their baptismal commitment in the midst of society, through their daily activity in family, social and professional life, and that they seek to develop new and creative means of evangelization. Many of these communities give a privileged place to the poor or marginal in society, to those who are wounded or living with

---

23. Cf. Directory, n. 69.
24. Cf. Directory, n. 52.

a handicap.[25] Each in its own way can give new expression to a shared discipleship in Jesus Christ.

Communities or movements can

- develop forms of shared ecumenical commitment in social, political and cultural life, by virtue of their lay character and the locus of their activity;
- seek appropriate avenues of jointly proclaiming and spreading the Gospel of Jesus Christ in various contexts;
- create opportunities for laity and clergy of different traditions to gather, pray and work together in an ecumenical spirit;
- organize ecumenical formation programs, weekends of spiritual recollection, seminars on Christian life;
- offer to Christians of different traditions a means of giving authentic expression to their real though imperfect unity in Christ, while respecting and even strengthening their rootedness in their own Christian communities.

---

25. E.g., L'Arche communities; the ATD (*Aide à Toute Détresse*) Fourth World Movement.

Young People

52. Each new generation of young Christians inherits the burden of past divisions. Their human and spiritual education is often marked, consciously or unconsciously, by prejudices and misunderstandings of divided Christian communities. It is confusing to hear the one message of the Gospel through many conflicting voices. Therefore it is of paramount importance that young Christians be given the opportunity to make friends with Christians of other traditions, to read the Gospel and to pray with them, to grow in understanding and appreciation of their particular gifts. However humble and small-scale these shared experiences may be, they are genuine steps toward greater unity among Christians.

As a consequence of secularization and also of Christian disunity, many young people today grow up with only a feeble sense of their Christian identity and a weak connection to their own ecclesial tradition. The individual traditions of Churches and Ecclesial Communities and distinctions between them tend to become blurred or irrelevant for them. To create possibilities for young people to rediscover authentic Christian community and the rich patrimony of Christian faith is becoming an increasingly important challenge shared by all Churches and Ecclesial Communities.

Together, young Christians can

- meet locally in small groups to deepen their faith and grow in a shared commitment to Jesus Christ;
- work together for reconciliation among their peers, in those regions where relations between Christians are troubled by the effects of recent conflicts;
- engage together in activities of spiritual ecumenism which are particularly adapted to young people, such as vigils, pilgrimages or youth camps;
- take part in programs of exchange, organized between Christian schools, universities or youth movements;
- attend meetings or events organized by particular communities or movements, that bring together young Christians from different regions and ecclesial traditions.[26]

---

26. E.g. the Community of Taizé, the Focolare Movement, the Sant' Egidio Community, the Chemin Neuf Community.

Pastoral Ministers

53. The Second Vatican Council entrusted the ecumenical task to bishops throughout the world, for their diligent promotion and prudent guidance.[27] Priests, deacons and all other pastoral agents, each in their own sphere, share in this ecumenical responsibility of the bishop. The pursuit of unity among Christians enters pastoral ministry in diverse ways, many of which have been identified above. This undertaking also touches each pastoral minister's own spirituality and personal way of relating to ministers of other traditions. Friendly and fraternal relations between pastoral ministers of different traditions are a primary means of promoting a spirituality of communion. The example given by their pastoral ministers is the most convincing teaching that the faithful can receive in matters of Christian unity.

Pastoral ministers can
- meet with ministers of other traditions for times of prayer and fraternal exchange at

---

27. UR, n. 4.

the local level, on a regular basis or at key moments of the liturgical year;[28]

- take part in national or international meetings for pastoral ministers of different traditions, such as those organized by a number of monastic communities, ecclesial communities or movements;[29]
- show solidarity when something important happens in the private or pastoral life of ministers of other traditions living in the same local area;
- foster relations with ministers of other traditions on the level of parish, diocese and region which give evidence of mutual trust, concern, and above all, a shared love of Christ and the Church.

---

28. E.g., Catholic and Orthodox bishops of particular cities in the East or in the West, who meet regularly; the annual meetings of Catholic and Anglican bishops in some regions to discuss relevant pastoral issues.
29. E.g., the ecumenical meeting of bishops "friends of the Focolare Movement"; the ecumenical meetings for bishops and clergy, organized by the Sant'Egidio Community.

Conclusion

54. With the Decree on Ecumenism of the Second Vatican Council, this Handbook on Spiritual Ecumenism can conclude that the *"holy task of reconciling all Christians in the unity of the one and only Church of Christ transcends human energies and abilities,"* and that therefore we should place our hope *"entirely in the prayer of Christ for the Church, in the love of the Father for us, and in the power of the Holy Spirit. 'And hope does not disappoint, because the charity of God is poured forth in our hearts by the Holy Spirit who has been given to us' (Rom 5:5)."*[1]

---

1. UR, n. 24.

Abbreviations

CCC: Catechism of the Catholic Church, 1994.

CCEO: Code of Canon Law of the Eastern Churches, 1990.

CIC: Code of Canon Law, 1983.

Directory: Pontifical Council for Promoting Christian Unity, *Directory for the Application of Principles and Norms on Ecumenism,* 1993.

DS: Denzinger-Schönmetzer, *Enchiridion Symbolorum,* 1976.

DV: Second Vatican Council, Dogmatic Constitution on Divine Revelation *Dei Verbum,* 1965.

EDE: Pope John Paul II, Encyclical Letter *Ecclesia de Eucharistia,* 2003.

IS: Pontifical Council for Promoting Christian Unity, *Information Service* bulletin.

LG: Second Vatican Council, Dogmatic Constitution on the Church *Lumen Gentium,* 1964.

NMI: Pope John Paul II, Apostolic Letter *Novo Millennio Ineunte,* 2001.

OE: Second Vatican Council, Decree on Eastern Catholic Churches, *Orientalium Ecclesiarum,* 1964.

OL: Pope John Paul II, Apostolic Letter *Orientale Lumen,* 1995.

RM: Pope John Paul II, Encyclical Letter *Redemptoris Mater,* 1990.

RS: Congregation for Divine Worship and the Discipline of Sacraments, Instruction *Redemptoris Sacramentum,* 2004.

SC: Second Vatican Council, Constitution on the Sacred Liturgy *Sacrosanctum Concilium,* 1963.

TMA: Pope John Paul II, Apostolic Letter *Tertio Millennio Adveniente,* 1994.

UR: Second Vatican Council, Decree on Ecumenism *Unitatis Redintegratio,* 1964.

UUS: Pope John Paul II, Encyclical Letter *Ut Unum Sint,* 1995.

VC: Pope John Paul II, Apostolic Exhortation *Vita Consecrata,* 1996.

Bibliography

Ecumenical Documents

This listing includes documents which are the result of international ecumenical dialogues in which the Catholic Church has been involved and which relate to particular aspects of "Spiritual Ecumenism." This list therefore does not mention all ecumenical documents of major importance, nor does it reflect their particular doctrinal authority; some documents have been officially approved by the competent authorities of the Catholic Church, while others are still part of an ongoing process of study and dialogue. Since many documents deal with a variety of inter-connected issues, the following classification is tentative; several documents could be listed under different headings.

Most documents can be found in the *Information Service* bulletin of the *Pontifical Council for Promoting Christian Unity*; in *Growth in Agreement I,* Reports and Agreed Statements of Ecumenical Conversations on a World Level, ed. H. Meyer and L. Vischer; and in *Growth in Agreement II,* 1982-1998, ed. J. Gros, H. Meyer and W. G. Rusch.[2]

---

2. All documents involving the Catholic Church on an international level can also be found on the website of the *Centro Pro Unione:* www.prounione.urbe.it.

Ecumenical documents on matters of faith:

- Common Declarations on Christology and other doctrinal issues, jointly signed or approved by the Bishop of Rome and Heads of particular Oriental Orthodox Churches (jointly signed, e.g., by Pope Paul VI and Patriarch Pope Shenouda III in 1973; by Pope Paul VI and Patriarch Mar Ignatius Jacoub III in 1971; by Pope John Paul II and Patriarch Mar Ignatius Zakka I Iwas in 1984 ; by Pope John Paul II and Catholicos Karekin I of All Armenians (Etchmiadzin) in 1996; by Pope John Paul II and Catholicos Aram I of Cilicia in 1997; jointly approved, e.g., by Pope John Paul II and Catholicos Baselios Mar Thoma Mathews II in 1990).

- Common Christological Declaration signed in 1994 by Pope John Paul II and Patriarch Mar Dinkha, Head of the Assyrian Church of the East.

- *The Notion of the "Hierarchy of Truths"*: *An Ecumenical Interpretation,* World Council of Churches–Catholic Church, Joint Working Group, 1990.

- *The Word of Life: A Statement on Revelation and Faith* (Rio Report), Methodist–Catholic Dialogue, 1996.

- *All Under One Christ,* Lutheran–Catholic Dialogue, 1980.

- *Joint Declaration on the Doctrine of Justification*, Lutheran–Catholic Dialogue, Augsburg, Germany, 1999. This text has been officially approved, and with the agreement of the

Congregation for the Doctrine of the Faith, was signed in 1999 by Cardinal Edward Cassidy and Bishop Walter Kasper on behalf of the Catholic Church; Bishop Christian Krause and Dr. Ishmael Noko, along with other Lutheran representatives, signed on behalf of the Lutheran World Federation. The World Methodist Council became officially associated with the Joint Declaration in 2006.

- *Confessing the One Faith: An Ecumenical Explication of the One Faith;* World Council of Churches, Commission on Faith and Order, 1999.

Ecumenical documents on the sacraments, particularly the sacraments of initiation:

- *Eucharistic Doctrine* (Windsor Statement), Anglican–Catholic Dialogue, 1971; *Elucidation*, 1979.
- *Vers une même foi eucharistique?,* Groupe des Dombes, 1972.[3]
- *The Theology of Marriage and the Problem of Mixed Marriages,* Lutheran-Reformed-Catholic Dialogue, 1976.
- *The Eucharist,* Lutheran–Catholic Dialogue, 1978.
- *Le Saint-Esprit, l'Eglise et les Sacrements*, Groupe des Dombes, 1976.
- *Baptism, Eucharist and Ministry* (BEM), World Council of Churches, Commission on Faith

---

3. The texts ot the *Groupe des Dombes* are the result of an unofficial dialogue involving Catholic and Protestant theologians, with an Orthodox presence.

and Order, 1982; *The Catholic Response to BEM,* 1988.

- *The Mystery of the Church and of the Eucharist in the Light of the Mystery of the Holy Trinity,* Orthodox–Catholic Dialogue, Munich, Germany, 1982.
- *Faith, Sacraments and the Unity of the Church,* Orthodox–Catholic Dialogue, Bari, Italy, 1987.
- *Ecclesiological and Ecumenical Implications of a Common Baptism,* World Council of Churches–Catholic Church, Joint Working Group, 2005.

Ecumenical documents on the Church:

- *Ways to Community,* Lutheran–Catholic Dialogue, 1980.
- *Salvation and the Church,* Anglican–Catholic Dialogue, 1987.
- *Towards a Statement on the Church* (Nairobi Report), Methodist–Catholic Dialogue, 1986.
- *Pour la communion des Eglises,* Groupe des Dombes, 1988.
- *Perspectives on Koinonia,* Pentecostal–Catholic Dialogue, 1985-1989.
- *Towards a Common Understanding of the Church,* Reformed–Catholic Dialogue, Second phase, 1984-1990.
- *The Church Local and Universal,* World Council of Churches–Catholic Church, Joint Working Group, 1990.
- *Church as Communion,* Anglican–Catholic Dialogue, 1991.

- *Pour la conversion des Eglises,* Groupe des Dombes, 1991.
- *The Church as Communion in Christ,* Disciples of Christ–Catholic Dialogue, St. Louis, Missouri, USA, 1992.
- *The Church in the Light of the Doctrine of Justification,* Lutheran–Catholic Dialogue, 1993.
- *Church, Evangelization and the Bonds of Koinonia,* Evangelical–Catholic Dialogue, 1993-2002.
- *The Nature and the Mission of the Church,* World Council of Churches, Commission on Faith and Order, 2005.
- *The Grace Given You in Christ: Catholics and Methodists Reflect Further on the Church* (Seoul Report), Methodist–Catholic Dialogue, 2006.

Ecumenical documents on Mary and the Communion of Saints:

- *Mary: Grace and Hope in Christ* (Seattle Statement), Anglican–Catholic Dialogue, 2005.
- *Marie dans le dessein de Dieu et la communion des saints,* Groupe des Dombes, 1997-1998.
- *Communio Sanctorum. Die Kirche als Gemeinschaft der Heiligen,* Deutsche Bishofskonferenz-VELKD, 2000.

Ecumenical documents on mission and common witness:

- *Dublin Report,* Methodist–Catholic Dialogue, 1976.
- *Summons to Witness to Christ in Today's World,* Baptist–Catholic Conversations, 1984-1988.

- *Dialogue on Mission,* Evangelical–Catholic Dialogue, 1977-1984.
- *Evangelisation, Proselytism and Common Witness,* Pentecostal–Catholic Dialogue, 1990-1997.
- *The Challenge of Proselytism and the Calling to Common Witness,* World Council of Churches–Catholic Church, Joint Working Group, 1995.
- *Receiving and Handing on the Faith: the Mission and Responsibility of the Church,* Disciples of Christ–Catholic Dialogue, 2002.

Ecumenical documents on life in Christ:

- *The Presence of Christ in Church and World, Final Report,* Reformed–Catholic Dialogue, 1977.
- *Life in Christ: Morals, Communion and the Church,* Anglican–Catholic Dialogue, 1994.
- *The Ecumenical Dialogue on Moral Issues: Potential Sources of Common Witness or of Divisions,* World Council of Churches–Catholic Church, Joint Working Group, 1995.

Ecumenical documents on the Holy Spirit and the Christian Community:

- *Final Report,* Pentecostal–Catholic Dialogue, 1972-1976.
- *Toward an Agreed Statement on the Holy Spirit* (Honolulu Report), Methodist–Catholic Dialogue, 1981.